D0116083

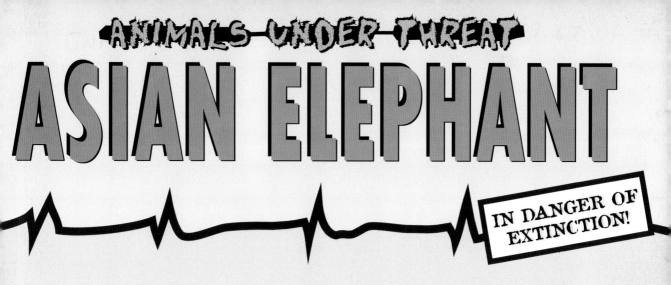

ANIMALS UNDER THREAT

ASIAN ELEPHANT

IN DANGER OF EXTINCTION!

Matt Turner

Heinemann Library
Chicago, Illinois

Customer Service 888–454–2279

Visit our website at www.heinemannlibrary.com

Photo research by Laura Durman
Designed by Ian Winton and Jo Malivoire
Printed in China by WKT Company Limited

09 08 07 06 05
10 9 8 7 6 5 4 3 2 1

Library of Congress Cataloging-in-Publication Data
Turner, Matt, 1964-
  Asian elephant / Matt Turner.
    p. cm. – (Animals under threat)
Includes bibliographical references and index.
  ISBN 1-4034-5581-3 (lib. bdg.) , 1-4034-5688-7 (pbk.)
1. Asiatic elephant – Juvenile literature. 2. Endangered species – Juvenile literature. I. Title
  QL737.P98 T87 2004
599.67/6 22   2004000573

Acknowledgments
The author and publisher are grateful to the following for permission to reproduce copyright material: Alamy pp. **7** (C. Fredriksson), **41** (D. Simpson); ardea.com pp. **16**, **21** (J. Rajput), **18**, **25**, **40** (J. Van Gruisen), **27** (P. Cavendish), **36** (T. & P. Leeson); Bruce Coleman p. **17** (J. P. Zwaenepoel); FLPA pp. **5** (D. Hosking), **13**, **20** (Silvestris), **28** (K. Rushford), **31** (G. Marcoaldi), **34** (M. Newman); Gerald Cubitt pp. **9**, **10**, **38**, **43**; NHPA pp. **12** (N. Garbutt), **14** (K. Schafer), **30** (A. & S. Toon), **35** (E. Janes), **39** (D. Heuclin); OSF pp. **22** (V. Sinha), **29** (A. Desai); Still pp. **15**, **23**, **24** (R. Seitre), **26** (M. Edwards), **32** (J. Etchart), **33** (M. Gunther); www.thetravel story.com p. **11** (P. S. Kristensen). Special thanks to IFAW for the image on page **42**.

Cover photograph reproduced with permission of Mary Plage (OSF) and Photodisc.

Some words are shown in bold, **like this.** You can find out what they mean by looking in the glossary.

Contents

The Asian Elephant

The Asian elephant is one of nature's giants. The largest can weigh as much as 70 people, or up to 6 tons. The only land animal bigger than the Asian elephant is the African elephant.

Asian and African elephants are **mammals.** They are actually two separate **species,** which means that they cannot **breed** together and produce offspring. As well as being smaller and lighter than the African elephant, the Asian elephant also has more toenails on its hind feet, one fewer pair of ribs, and a greater number of bones in its back.

All species have a scientific name. The African elephant is known as *Loxodonta africana*, while the Asian elephant is called *Elephas maximus*. Scientists divide the Asian elephant population into five **subspecies**. These are *Elephas maximus maximus* (found in Sri Lanka), *Elephas maximus indicus* (found in India and Southeast Asia), *Elephas maximus sumatranus* (from Sumatra), and *Elephas maximus hirsutus* on the Malay **peninsula**. A fifth subspecies, the pygmy elephant of Borneo, has only recently been reported, and is not yet named. There are only small differences between the subspecies. *Elephas maximus hirsutus* is hairier than the others. The pygmy elephant is the smallest. It has straighter tusks and larger ears, and its tail is longer compared to its body size.

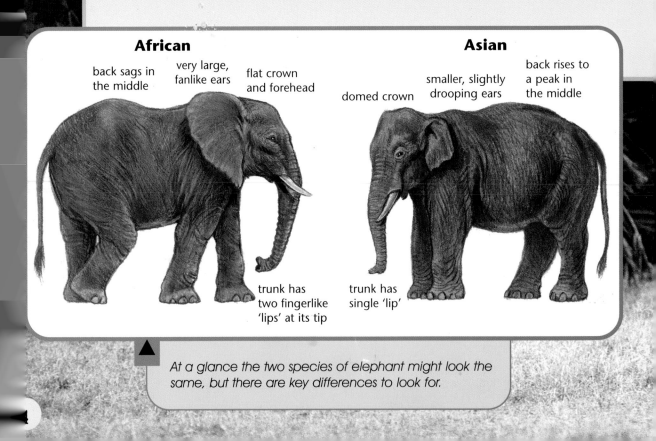

African

back sags in the middle

very large, fanlike ears

flat crown and forehead

Asian

domed crown

smaller, slightly drooping ears

back rises to a peak in the middle

trunk has two fingerlike 'lips' at its tip

trunk has single 'lip'

At a glance the two species of elephant might look the same, but there are key differences to look for.

In its cousin's shadow

Though both elephant species have grown rarer over the years, attention has focused mostly on the African elephant. It has been heavily hunted for its **ivory** tusks. In comparison, the Asian elephant has been largely ignored. There are many Asian elephants in captivity, so people tend to assume that they are not endangered. However, in the wild they are running out of space as people take over or change the elephants' natural **habitat.** If the world does not take steps to save it, the Asian elephant will quietly vanish from the wild.

Both the Asian elephant (above) and the African elephant are endangered.

Yesterday's giants

There are just two elephant species alive today, but once there were many. Their earliest ancestors lived in what is now south Asia and Africa, and spread to every continent on Earth except Antarctica and Australia. There were many different forms of elephant: some had shovel-like jaws, others had peg-like tusks.

Mammoths were long-tusked cousins of modern elephants. Some were huge, standing over 3 feet (1 meter) taller than a modern Asian elephant. The woolly mammoth lived in the north of the North American continent, Europe, and Asia. It had a shaggy coat to keep out cold weather and biting insects, and it probably fed on mosses and shrubs. We know what woolly mammoths looked like because their remains have been found, perfectly preserved, in ice. Mammoths died out about 10,000 years ago. Changes in climate and plant life may have killed them off. However, by that date humans were already hunting mammoths for their meat.

The Asian elephant once **ranged** over a large area of Asia. It was found from Syria and Iraq in the west, to Borneo in the east, and from the island of Sumatra in the south, to at least as far north as China's Yangtze (Chang Jiang) River. By 1000 C.E., the elephant had vanished from Syria, Iraq, Java, and most of southern China.

The Asian elephant is now found in 13 countries: India, Nepal, Bangladesh, Bhutan, Sri Lanka, Myanmar (Burma), Thailand, Malaysia, Indonesia, Laos, Cambodia, Vietnam, and China. India, Sri Lanka, Bhutan, Nepal, and Bangladesh contain over 60 percent of all Asia's wild elephants. Cambodia, China, Laos, and Vietnam together account for less than 5 percent.

ant distribution today

*Scattered blocks are all that remain of the elephant's **range** across mainland and island Asia.*

Broken distribution

If you gathered together all the plots of land occupied by Asian elephants, you would end up with a total area of nearly 193,000 square miles (500,000 square kilometers). This is an area a little smaller than France. Before lots of people began to settle in India, around 3000 B.C.E., the elephant had a stable population on the mainland. Today, as the map shows, this population is broken up into separate pieces.

Elephants have vanished completely from central India. In the rest of India, elephant numbers are down to 25,000 in all the interior and northwestern states. Their largest populations are scattered through the hill regions of the southwest (9,600 to 15,200 animals) and the northeast (about 6,800 animals). Small populations are strung out in blocks along the Himalayan foothills. In Myanmar (Burma) and Thailand, populations are similarly scattered. Each block is itself broken down into many tiny, separate portions.

Chinese elephants

In ancient China, most peasant farmers saw elephants as a threat to their land and their crops. A ruler in 1105 B.C.E. is said to have driven away "the tiger, leopard, rhinoceros, and elephant to the great joy of the people." As they cleared the ancient forests and planted crops, over thousands of years, Chinese peasants steadily pushed elephants southward. Today there are about 300 elephants left in China.

Human help

In rare cases, human acts have helped spread the Asian elephant's population. In the Andaman Islands in the Bay of Bengal, there are 20 to 30 elephants. They are from a tiny population introduced there as working animals in the **logging** industry.

The pygmy elephant was trapped on the island of Borneo when sea levels rose long ago. As time passed, its appearance and behavior changed. It is now different from other kinds of elephant.

A new elephant

In September 2003 scientists analyzing elephant **DNA** announced that Borneo's elephants are a separate **subspecies** of Asian elephant. It had once been thought that the island's elephants had died out in **prehistoric** times, and the current population was descended from elephants given as a present to a local ruler in 1750. This has been proved wrong. Scientists now say that the elephants have been cut off from other Asian populations for about 300,000 years. During this time, they have evolved into a different elephant—one that is smaller and less aggressive.

The total population of Asian elephants that lived in the wild in 1900 is thought to have been 100,000. Today there are between 34,500 and 51,000. Most researchers think the true population is about 45,000 to 48,000. There are another 16,000 or so elephants in captivity. This is a tiny fraction of the total numbers that have been captured throughout recorded history: an estimated 2 to 4 million elephants, including about 100,000 just in the past 100 years.

Population totals are falling throughout Asia, but the rate of decline varies from one region to another. Some of the hardest-hit regions are in southeast Asia. One 2002 report revealed that, since 1990, elephant numbers have dropped by more than 90 percent in Vietnam, by nearly 90 percent in Cambodia, and by 50 percent in Laos, a nation once known as the Land of a Million Elephants. In Thailand, within the past 20 years, the elephant population might have declined by 50 percent.

Population chart

These numbers show the approximate minimum, maximum, and probable Asian elephant population counts for each region.

Region	Minimum number of elephants	Probable number of elephants	Maximum number of elephants
India	19,100	24,300	29,450
Nepal	40	50	60
Bangladesh	200	220	240
Bhutan	60	80	100
Sri Lanka	3,200	3,800	4,400
Myanmar	4,600	4,800	5,000
Thailand	1,300	1,700	2,000
Malaysia	800	1,000	1,200
Borneo	1,000	1,300	1,500
Indonesia	2,800	3,800	4,800
Laos	1,000	1,100	1,300
Cambodia	200	250	500
Vietnam	100	140	145
China	250	280	300
Total	**34,650**	**42,820**	**50,995**

Islands of elephants

The breaking up of its population is one of the most serious threats facing the elephant today. Human settlements form barriers that split elephant country into fragments. Elephant populations are divided into small groups that cannot mix with one another. Adult elephants find it increasingly hard to find a **mate** at **breeding** time.

If there are fewer than 500 animals of a specific **species,** the species does not have a good chance of surviving. This is because if there are fewer than 500 animals the animals in the group are too closely related. If the animals in a group are closely related, they can all fall ill from the same cause. A small population can easily be wiped out by disease.

Complicated counting

Scientists are unsure of how many elephants there actually are because elephants are surprisingly hard to count! They are easily hidden in the forests where they live. Also, many populations live on national borders where political problems make it difficult to do surveys. So, field researchers have to be creative. To avoid counting the same animal twice, they look for odd features, such as broken or twisted tusks, or torn ears. To be able to tell one elephant from another they also look at size. Researchers can calculate an animal's height from a photograph. Footprints are useful, too. An elephant's shoulder height is approximately twice the **circumference** of its forefoot. Another method involves measuring the amount of dung in a given area. It is messy, but very helpful, since the dung is also used in other scientific tests.

▶ This elephant only has one tusk. Special features like this help researchers count elephant populations accurately.

The Asian elephant can survive almost anywhere as long as there are trees to shelter it from the hot sun. It is at home in marshes, bamboo forests, palm tree **thickets,** and grassy **scrub.** It is even found in the Himalayan foothills, where there are freezing nighttime temperatures.

The thickest elephant populations are found in dry, thorny scrub forest where there is a single annual **monsoon** (wet season) giving 24 to 79 inches (60 to 200 centimeters) of rainfall. Dry scrub forest is common in southern India and Sri Lanka.

Tropical rain forest covers much of southeast Asia, including most of the Malay **peninsula.** Undisturbed rain forest contains few elephants. It is too **humid,** and food plants are too widely scattered. Rain forest that has been opened up a little by humans, but not destroyed, is better. It contains regular sunlit clearings where food plants for elephants can grow.

River deep, mountain high

Elephants must drink plenty and often, so they need to live near a good source of water. The **floodplains** of major Asian rivers, as well as countless smaller waterways, once swarmed with elephants.

Elephants need water. This lake in southwest India was created in 1895 to provide hunting grounds for the British, but today it lies at the heart of a wildlife sanctuary.

Unfortunately an elephant's ideal home is similar to ours. The first places humans settled in Asia were fertile, wooded, and grassy floodplains. People pushed the elephants out. Today, elephants are concentrated mostly in hilly regions, such as the Western and Eastern Ghats of southern India, the Dangreks on the Thailand/Cambodia border, and the Cardamom and Elephant Mountains in Cambodia. Hill **ranges** are typically the last types of terrain to be settled or cultivated by people.

Home on the range

Elephants are constantly on the move from one day to the next, and from one season to another, in search of food, water, shelter, or each other. The area of land to which each elephant herd keeps, and which contains all the elephants' needs, is called a **home range.** The size of a home range varies, depending on whether **resources** are widely scattered or not, and whether the animals are free to roam or are blocked in by dams, villages, and crops. The range may measure from 8 sq miles (20 sq kilometers) up to 230 sq miles (600 sq kilometers). The size depends on the time of year, and can be three times bigger during the dry season. Regularly used forests become laced with elephant paths and dotted with clearings in which they gather.

Measuring range

Space technology helps us measure elephant ranges through use of the global positioning system (GPS). Researchers fit **radio transmitters** to **tranquilized** elephants that are then released back into the wild. The transmitter sends a signal to a **satellite** in space. The satellite beams the signal back to a receiver and computer on Earth showing exactly where the animal is. The researchers use the GPS data to calculate how far each individual elephant roams. By tracking several different elephants, they can monitor seasonal movements and calculate an average home range figure.

Asian elephants are true giants. The limb joints are arranged for carrying loads, not for running fast. The elephant usually walks at about 2 to 2.5 miles (3 to 4 kilometers) per hour. However, it can charge at up to 25 miles (40 kilometers) per hour. It is the only land **mammal** that cannot jump.

Body basics

An elephant's trunk is really an elongated upper lip and nose with the two nostrils at its tip. It can function as a hand for picking up seeds, tearing out trees, or touching another elephant tenderly. It can sniff the air for distant scents or deliver a wide range of calls. It is also a hose for sucking up and squirting out water.

Teeth and tusks

An elephant's tusks are overgrown teeth. The **ivory** is a dense, hard material, called dentine. Bulls, or male elephants, have long tusks, while cows, or female elephants, have stubby, down-curving tusks, known as tushes. Not all bulls have tusks. Whether they do or not depends partly on where they live. In Cambodia, almost none have tusks,while in southern India over 90 percent do. Overall, 1 in 10 Asian elephants (male and female) have tusks.

*The male Asian elephant, or bull, has much longer tusks than the female. The heavy **poaching** that continues to this day means that magnificent tusks like these are now rarely seen.*

An elephant has 24 back teeth during its lifetime. As the teeth wear out they break up, and others slowly move forward to replace them. By the age of 30 to 40 the elephant is using its final, sixth set of **molars.** These are great, brick-sized teeth that each weigh up to 8 pounds (3.5 kilograms). When these go, by the age of 50 to 60, the elephant starves to death because it cannot chew.

An elephant's trunk, which can hold several gallons of water, is useful for soaking the skin as well as for drinking.

Air supply

An elephant needs plenty of oxygen to fuel its huge body. People think that oxygen starvation is a common cause of death in captive elephants. The harder a body works, the more oxygen it needs in its blood. The elephant's heart muscles take in oxygen quite slowly. If an elephant is overworked, its heart simply does not get enough oxygen to keep up.

Keeping cool

Losing body heat is extremely important to an elephant, but it has no sweat **glands.** Provided its skin stays wet, water will **evaporate** from it, taking body heat away. That is why an elephant likes to wallow in rivers or slap on wet mud. When there is no water available, it may use its trunk to suck moisture from its mouth and spray this over its skin. In ideal conditions, about a gallon (4 to 5 liters) of water evaporates from an adult's body every hour. An elephant also uses its ears to stay cool. The body's heat is carried to a network of blood vessels lining the ears. The elephant flaps its ears to make air currents that draw the heat away. In a breeze, the elephant simply sticks its ears straight out.

Size basics

Head & body length	18–21 ft (5.4–6.4m)
Tail length	4–5 ft (1.2–1.5 m)
Male shoulder height	8–10 ft (2.5–3 m)
Average male weight	5.3 tons (5.4 metric tons)

Silent step

Despite its size an elephant can move quietly. Its weight is spread over a large area. An elephant's total footprint (the area of ground covered by all four soles) is about nine sq feet (one sq meter). Beneath the elephant's foot bones are thick soles of fat that act like cushions, muffling the cracking of sticks. Each sole spreads out under the weight, then shrinks again on lifting, so the feet do not get stuck in mud.

Food and Feeding

Elephants are herbivores, or vegetarians. This means that they do not eat meat. They eat a mixed diet of grasses and **browse** (the name for the leaves, woody twigs, and bark from trees and shrubs). They also eat fruits, flowers, and roots. Increasingly, elephants feed on planted crops, and this is a serious cause of conflict with farmers.

Varying diet

Across their **range,** Asian elephants select from as many as 400 different plant **species.** What they eat, and when they eat it, varies from one region to another. In a study in southern India, browse made up 70 percent of the elephants' diet during the January–April dry season. In the heavy May–June rains, the elephants ate fresh grasses, which made up 54 percent of their diet. The elephants moved from one food source to another. During the rainy months they spread out into grassy areas. In dry months they clustered in river valleys.

Daily dining

Elephants have giant appetites. An adult usually eats over 220 pounds (100 kilograms) of food per day, but can eat 3 times that if hungry. To take in its mighty meals, the elephant must feed morning, afternoon, and night for about 14 hours in every 24. Usually it rests in the midday heat.

Asian elephants browse on tree parts. Some trees die as a result, but others are stimulated into sending out new growth.

Packing its trunk

The Asian elephant uses its trunk to collect food and pass it to its mouth. It curls the trunk around long grasses and rips them up. It may use its forefeet to hold **vegetation** down while ripping, and to kick and loosen tufts of grass. To strip bark from branches, an elephant uses its trunk tip to twist the branch against its teeth. To pick up fruits and seeds from the ground, the elephant delicately dabs each onto the tip of its trunk.

The Asian elephant is a thirsty drinker. It drinks about 20 gallons (90 liters) of water a day. The elephant's trunk can hold just over a gallon (5to 6 liters) of water at one time. It usually drinks every day at least once, but can go several days without water if necessary. Elephants are experts at finding hidden water. In long dry spells they kick at dried-up riverbeds, allowing groundwater to well up into the holes they dig. They can smell rain from several miles away.

Help with digestion

Almost half of an elephant's food passes straight through the **gut** and into the dung, without being **digested** at all. This is because the elephant's gut, where digestion takes place, is relatively short. Help, however, is given by tiny **organisms,** called microorganisms. They live in the elephant's gut and help break down the food.

Seed sowers

Elephants do not just take food. They help to grow it, too. When they eat plant seeds, the seeds often pass undigested through the elephant's warm gut. By the time they are passed out again in dung, the hard seed cases are usually softened. The softening and warmth encourage the seed to **germinate** quickly. By moving a seed from the shade of its parent tree to another part of forest, an elephant also helps spread its food plants around.

Asian Elephant Groups

Elephants are social animals. They live in herds. This habit helps young elephants learn essential survival skills from their elders.

Strong bond

The bond between a cow (female) and her young is so strong that calves stay close to their mother even into their teens. Cow–calf units form the basic building blocks of herds that today usually number 15 to 40 animals. The cows are fiercely protective of their young, and form a defensive ring around them if threatened by danger. In fact, adult elephants' only **predators** are people, though tigers may attack calves.

Cows grow up and stay in the same herd as their mother, even when they, too, begin to breed. The three young elephants in this group belong to an old cow and her adult daughter.

Young males, or bulls, gradually separate from the family when they are between 12 and 20 years old. They then either live alone or join loose-knit **bachelor** herds with other bulls until they are old enough to **breed.** Bachelor herds usually have up to 8 animals. Once they reach breeding age, bulls live alone. When bulls want to **mate,** they seek out a herd. At any one time, one third to one half of all cow-calf herds are also accompanied by at least one lone bull in search of a mate.

Super herds

Sometimes several small, related herds join togethe[r]
These are known as bond families. Larger groups ar[e]
known as clans. These are mass seasonal groupings,
often involved with **migration** and probably cause[d]
a joint search for water or food. Clans once contain[ed]
thousands of elephants, but usually number in the
hundreds today.

Herd sizes

The great variation in
herd size is explained
partly by differences
in **habitat** and food
supply. Prime **floodplain** grassland—grass enriched by the flooding of
nearby rivers—in southern India may support up to 8 elephants per
square mile, while **tropical** forest in Malaysia may support only 1
elephant per 27 square miles (70 square kilometers), and therefore
much smaller herds. Herds often break down into smaller groups of
cow-calf units when there are changes in the environment.

Female leader

Cows may spend their whole life in the herd in which they were born.
This means that the eldest herd member is always female. She is
usually between 40 and 60 years old. Her age has given her a store of
knowledge. She is known as the **matriarch.** Her skills and her stored
memories of where to find food, shelter, and water are essential to the
herd's survival.

In times of danger the matriarch guides the group to
safety. Unfortunately this puts her at most risk of attack
from hunters. If a matriarch is shot dead, her herd
becomes confused. The members may try to push her
body upright again or simply stand about it,
trumpeting, unsure of what to do next. For this
reason, hunters often shoot deliberately at what they
think is the
matriarch. When a
matriarch dies of
natural causes,
herds break down
into smaller units
of cows and their
calves. The next
most senior cow
may then take
over the role
of matriarch.

*Groups of cows and th[eir]
calves form a herd at
Nagarhole National Pa[rk,]
India. Tigers are now s[o rare]
that this is one of the fe[w]
places where elephan[ts and]
tigers share living space*

On the Move

As their diet changes from one season to the next, so elephants move from one food source to another. They also move in response to changing rainfall patterns. This seasonal movement is known as **migration.**

Following the seasons

Elephant expert Dr. Raman Sukumar studied an elephant population in the Biligirirangan hills of southern India from 1981 to 1982. He found that during the dry months of January to April, elephants clustered in a forested river valley. It offered shade and a reliable source of water and **browse.**

After the May to August rains, most of the elephants spread out into higher, more open country to graze on tall grasses. With the onset of heavier, **monsoon** rains in September, the animals moved down into areas containing shorter grasses or dry thorn forest, remaining there until December. Shifting food sources are not the only reason for migration. Forest fires force elephants to move out of an area, though they often return as soon as green shoots spring from the scorched soil. Biting flies and flooded ground are other annoyances that make elephants move.

Asian elephants, unlike African elephants, usually travel single file through woodland, especially where the land is hilly. Their paths have often been used by many generations of elephants.

Follow the leader

Some elephant herds move as unpredictably as the weather. Others follow traditional routes (and become easy targets for hunters). The herd is led from the front by the **matriarch.** Long experience has taught her where water sources lie, how food sources shift through the year, and so on. This knowledge is passed down from one generation to the next within each herd.

Regional range

Asian elephants do not travel as much as their African cousins. In Africa, annual round trips of up to 500 miles (800 kilometers) in Mali and 125 miles (200 kilometers) in Botswana have been observed. A typical seasonal movement in Asia is 10 to 30 miles (20 to 50 kilometers.) Differences in the terrain, climate, and **vegetation** of each continent are partly responsible.

Within Asia, elephants migrate in regions where seasonal change is more obvious. In **tropical rain forest,** where seasons do not differ so much, elephants do not need to migrate at certain times of the year. So while elephants regularly move up to 30 miles (50 kilometers) from one feeding site to another in the hills of southern India, they do not migrate at all on the Malay **peninsula,** an area of tropical forest.

No through road

Today, Asian elephants find that traditional migration routes throughout their **range** have been blocked by human settlements. This leads to conflict when the animals stray across farm land in attempts to follow their traditional road map.

Nose to tail, a herd of elephants follows its female leader into river shallows before spreading out to drink and bathe.

Elephants use smell, sound, gestures, and touch to communicate with each other and to detect threats. Their sense of smell is superb. It is common to see elephants raise their trunks and wave them about in order to locate a strange scent. Elephants also produce scent, through chemicals in their dung, urine, and breath. Each elephant in a herd gets to know the personal scent of all the herd members. This scent awareness comforts calves, reassures adults, and strengthens relationships. Scent plays an important role in **breeding,** too. Breeding bulls are especially smelly, and the odor warns nonbreeding bulls not to approach them. Scent also helps bulls to detect females that are ready to **mate.**

An elephant raises its trunk. This is a threat display, but it is also a good way of sniffing the air to test another animal's scent and find out whether or not it is friendly.

Calling all elephants

In a forest, however, airborne scent does not travel as far as sound, and elephants use a wide range of calls. These include a deep growl which can be heard by other elephants up to half a mile away. It is used partly to show happiness, but also to say "I am over here," especially when among trees. Elephants trumpet through their trunk when they are excited (such as when greeting relatives), angry, afraid, or just playing. A danger alert may be given with a low snort. A dramatic sound is the trunk boom, in which an elephant smacks the tip of its trunk on the ground to make an explosively loud sound. Gestures help an elephant establish its rank in the herd. A high-ranking elephant may carry its head high. A **submissive** animal may place the tip of its trunk into another's mouth. The sensitive tip is very important to an elephant, so placing it where it could be chewed off means trust and surrender. At all times, elephants in a herd love to touch each other with their trunks.

The trunk is used like a sensitive hand for feeling other animals. Everyday touching helps to strengthen friendships between members of a herd.

How low can they go?

In the 1980s scientist Dr. Katy Payne suggested that deep growling allows elephants to talk in infrasound, a noise that human ears cannot hear. We can hear sounds as low as 20 Hz (hertz, or vibrations per second). Elephants can hear as low as 14 Hz. Deep notes travel further than high ones. Their infrasonic rumbles may be heard from 5 miles (8 kilometers) away or even more. It explains how separate herds keep in touch when they cannot see one another. Infrasound may also give researchers a way of counting elephant populations. They can leave a microphone and tape recorder in elephant country to record the deep rumbling calls and use computer software to calculate how many animals are present.

Breeding

Elephants live for almost as long as we do, often reaching 60 or 70 years of age. However, they do not **breed** in a hurry. A bull is capable of reproducing from about 8 years of age, but he rarely does so until he is 20 or even 30 years old. This is because he must compete with other bulls for a **mate,** and to win he must be large and powerful.

*When a bull is in musth, his cheeks are stained with a fluid that leaks from **glands** on his head.*

Wandering bulls

Every year large adult bulls come into a breeding condition known as **musth.** The period of musth tends to occur at specific times of the year, depending on the location of the elephants, and lasts for nearly three months.

While in musth, a bull wanders widely in search of mates. If he runs into other bulls each bull shows off his size and strength by posturing, and by tusking, or thrashing at plants. Their dispute is usually settled without bloodshed. Smaller bulls always give way to large bulls, especially those in musth.

Musth madness

Musth is a word from India that means drunk. In fact, the bull is affected by a massive surge of the **hormone** testosterone that floods through his bloodstream at 50 times the normal level. The hormone makes him want to mate, and it also makes him aggressive. The mood changes are a necessary part of the mating process.

Capable cow

For about 4 days in every 22, a cow is in estrus. This means she is capable of becoming pregnant. Bulls in musth seek out cows in estrus to mate with. When a bull has won a cow, he guards her for a few days, and they mate a number of times. He leaves her when her estrus period ends.

Elephants are pregnant for almost two years. They give birth to one calf at a time. The calf is about 35 inches (90 centimeters) high at the shoulder and weighs over 198 pounds (90 kilograms). It has a coat of reddish or yellowish hair, but this soon falls out.

First steps

The calf is normally on its feet within a couple of hours, seeking its mother's milk. It suckles for a minute or so every 40 to 50 minutes, day and night. In every 24 hours the calf drinks up to 3 gallons (15 liters). At first the calf is awkward and unsure of how to use its trunk. The constant company of its mother and play with other calves help it learn as it grows.

For four or five years the calf never once leaves its mother's side. Though it starts to eat **vegetation** at a few months old, it may keep suckling throughout this period. The mother needs endless patience. She may also have one or two older calves with her. She may continue to have calves at two- to eight-year intervals until she is in her fifties. She also has to move more slowly than the rest of the herd. For this reason herds sometimes separate into smaller **crèches.**

Starting at seven or eight years old, a calf is happy to spend time away from its mother. Its physical growth is still rapid. At ten years old its growth slows down. At about 30 years of age the elephant has reached full height, though it may continue to gain weight.

A calf uses its mouth, not its trunk, to suckle from its mother, who must stand patiently. You can see the calf's birth coat of hair. This is shed as the animal grows.

Asian Elephants at Work

Highly intelligent, quick to learn commands, and capable of hauling more than half a ton, the Asian elephant has long served people in many different roles.

More than 5,000 years ago, settlers in the Indus Valley of India and Pakistan began taming elephants to help them clear wilderness areas. Over thousands of years tame elephants have been used for many duties: extracting logs from forests, plowing, and carrying people or cargo.

In parts of Asia, Elephants are still used to carry heavy burdens. This animal in Delhi, India, is carrying not only its rider, but also its packed lunch!

Royal stables

It became a tradition for nobles and royals to own elephants. Garlanded, painted, and jeweled, the animals played a starring role in royal and religious ceremonies, and carried their riders during tiger hunts. Indian rulers set up special reserves where wild elephants were to be captured unharmed. Anyone found killing them was put to death. The emperor Chandragupta, who ruled India from 321 to 297 B.C.E., is said to have owned 9,000 elephants.

Elephants at war

Asian elephants served in many ancient battles. In 331 B.C.E., Darius III of Persia set them against the Macedonian leader, Alexander the Great. Alexander was so impressed that he used elephants to invade India five years later. The use of war elephants continued in Asia for centuries. It declined with the widespread introduction of firearms in the 1500s. However, during World War II, the British army had an Elephant Company to help build bridges and haul equipment through the jungles of Burma (now Myanmar). In the Vietnam War United States warplanes bombed elephants to stop enemy forces from using the animals for transportation. However, elephants were far from ideal in battle. They were nervous and unpredictable, and might suddenly turn on their own soldiers and trample them.

Capture and training

Elephants are not easy to **breed** in captivity. Both sexes need space to roam at will when they are ready to **mate.** In the past it was simpler to capture new animals from the wild population. Early northern Indian peoples caught elephants in a kheddah, a timber stockade that whole herds were driven into by men making noise and waving torches. On a good day's hunt 50 or more could be rounded up. Tame elephants were often used in round-ups because of their calming effect on the wild herds. This practice was used across the Asian elephant's **range,** well into the mid-20th century. Another method involved driving elephants into water and then lassoing them by an ear. Farther south, hunters would trap smaller numbers in a large, deep pit.

Elephants can be taught to respond to basic commands within a few days. Usually it takes a week or so to get an elephant to kneel and take its rider, or **mahout.** Elephants may then learn to obey up to a hundred different commands.

In southern India ranks of elephants in colorful dress participate in religious ceremonies. This is the Pooram festival that takes place in Kerala every April.

Religious symbol

The Asian elephant is a sacred figure in some Asian religions. It features strongly in ancient Indian myths. Hindus worship the elephant-headed god Ganesh. Ganesh worship has helped protect wild elephants, since Hindus are reluctant to kill them. The elephant has been revered by Buddhists, too, since the third century B.C.E. In their texts the Buddha was reborn as a snow-white elephant with six tusks. Today elephants still play a role in religious festivals.

Losing Ground

In spite of its rich history, the Asian elephant has an uncertain future. The greatest threat today is the loss of its **habitat.** India's human population rose from 236 million in 1901 to over 1 billion in 2003. New people need new land, water, and food. Twentieth-century programs to get rid of **malaria**-carrying mosquitoes in the hills of southern India and the Himalayan foothills have allowed farmers to move in. Across Asia the picture is similar. A rising human population is taking over the remaining wildernesses. One estimate claims that, overall, the Asian elephant has lost up to 70 percent of its **range** since the 1960s.

Competing cattle

Keeping cattle in elephant habitat causes problems. The hooves of cattle compact the soil and stop water from soaking in. Cattle also carry diseases, such as anthrax or foot and mouth, which can spread to elephants. Cattle overgraze native plants such as bamboo. This allows weeds to invade and take over, reducing the elephants' food supply.

Spreading crops

Deforestation continues today at an alarming rate. **Native vegetation** is giving way to vast **plantations** of export crops, such as tea, coffee, sugar cane, cocoa, and bananas. In southern India, about ten percent of former elephant country has been lost to plantations of teak and silver oak (both hardwoods used to make furniture), wattle (used in the leather tanning industry), and eucalyptus (used to make plywood and paper pulp, among other things). Malaysia loses over two percent of its forest area each year.

Villagers in Thailand turn a scorched hillside into new crop land. The country, now heavily deforested, offers little habitat to wild elephants and little work for domestic forestry elephants.

Myanmar (Burma) is today one of the few Asian countries that still uses elephants in forestry. Most are put to work handling heavy logs of teak, a timber grown for furniture.

Faster shifting

Much of Asia's moist **tropical** forests are changing. Farmers cut or burn away the forest, then plant a few crops before moving on to a new site. In the farmers' absence, undergrowth is given time to reclaim the **fallow** land that still provides living space for local elephants. However, farmers are being crammed onto smaller and smaller plots. They are returning sooner to the fallow land. Farmers in southern India used to leave the land fallow for between ten and twenty years. Today they leave it for less than five years. As a result, the land becomes unproductive. The elephants have less living space because farmers are leaving less time between planting crops on the same land. This means that there is less time for elephant food plants to grow back.

Uprooted

Logging affects wild animals in many Asian countries. While governments and international associations make attempts to control logging companies, illegal logging continues regardless. Elephants have been used by loggers for years to clear the very forests they depend upon in the wild.

Asian Elephants and Farmers

About one fifth of the world's human population is found in, or very near, Asian elephant **habitat.** Millions of these people are very poor. They will go hungry or even starve if their crops and homes are damaged by elephants. Elephants, forced into smaller, isolated clumps of forest, sometimes stray into settlements. Farmers and villagers can come to see elephants as a neighborhood threat.

*Fields, like this coffee **plantation** in Vietnam, are no-go areas for elephants. But as more and more land goes under the plow, keeping animals off crops is getting harder.*

Crop raiders

Today, some of the crops elephants raid include millet, banana, rice, sugar cane, and oil palm. The elephants feed at night and trample the crops as they eat them. Sometimes a farmer's entire season's crop is destroyed. It is usually mature bulls, either alone or in small groups, that cause the trouble. They wander widely (especially when **breeding**) and are more likely to enter fields. Many bulls develop a taste for crop raiding. Cows tend not to raid crops for fear of putting their calves at risk.

Today, in most **range countries,** it is illegal to kill an elephant without a government license. Villagers can do little to protect their livelihood, but some take the law into their own hands. During 2001 in Assam in India, villagers poisoned 31 elephants to stop them from crop raiding. In Sri Lanka, an estimated 110 to 120 elephants are killed each year, mostly after elephants have raided crops.

Why raid crops?

Some elephants raid crops because the fields lie on their ancient home **range,** or because it is the best food available. Plants grown as crops are simply wild plants bred for centuries by humans to be tastier and more **nutritious.** In certain seasons, crops offer elephants more nutrition than wild grasses. Also, crops do not contain the toxins (poisons) produced by wild plants for self-defense against plant-eaters.

Dangerous elephants

Farmers try to shoo raiding elephants away with torches, guns, and firecrackers, but bulls are not easily scared, and they can be dangerous, too. Up to 150 people are killed by elephants every year in India alone. Many are trampled, gored, or hurled aside while trying to protect their crops, but often the victims are presenting no threat. Bulls in **musth,** or **matriarchs** trying to defend their herd, have been known to charge into villages and attack people. Sometimes they are simply startled by the bark of a dog.

Keeping elephants at bay

Farmers try various methods to protect their fields. Sometimes trenches are dug around crops. A simple soil trench tends to collapse after heavy rain, and elephants are good at crossing them. They simply kick at the top of the slopes until they fill the trench with soil and then cross it. Concrete trenches are too expensive for most farmers to build.

Buffer zones are belts of land that separate elephants from land used by humans. They may be planted with grasses that elephants enjoy, so that the animals eat their fill before they reach crops. Or the zones may be left clear, to deter elephants from crossing them. Buffer zones are only partly effective, and they use up a lot of land.

Another method is to put up an electric fence. This delivers a brief burst of very high voltage. It is effective, and over a given distance is about one-third the cost of trenching. But electric fences need maintenance and can be easily stolen by other farmers.

Elephants that keep on raiding crops run the risk of being shot by angry villagers. Some, too, are killed by eating poisoned bait left out for troublesome wild pigs.

Meat and Ivory

People hunt elephants for meat and their skin. The elephant skin is turned into bags and shoes. Skin and meat are both used in Chinese medicine. **Ivory poaching** occurs across the **range.** The trade in Asian elephant ivory is small compared with that in Africa. Asian elephants are fewer in number, harder to track, less likely to carry tusks, and spared by many people for religious reasons. Also, Asian cultures have a long tradition of using live elephants in daily life.

In areas where elephants have been raiding crops and damaging buildings, it becomes harder for authorities to control poaching. Villagers are more likely to kill elephants themselves, or to support the activities of poachers. If they try to stand up to poachers, they themselves might face death threats. Today's poachers are ruthless, organized gangs with guns. Government **wardens** are hired to combat the gangs, but wardens are expensive to hire, and finding people in the forest is difficult.

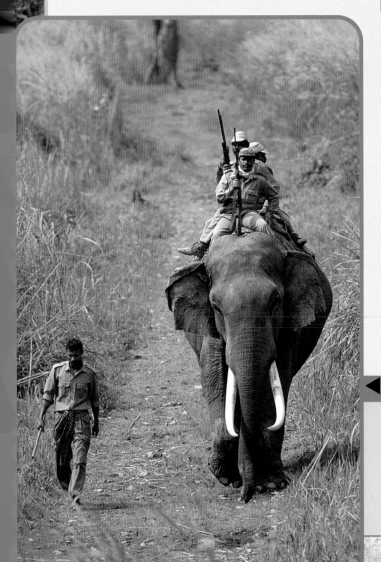

Ivory trade

Asia plays a key role in the world ivory market. India has a flourishing ivory carving industry, and for over 2,500 years African ivory has been shipped into the country to be carved, then sold in other parts of the world. Between 1979 and 1990 an estimated 700,000 African elephants—over half the total population—were killed for their tusks. The Asian carving industry grew rapidly to meet the demand.

Looking after its wild cousins: a domestic elephant carries a patrol in search of ivory poachers. The most successful patrols are those that include people with local knowledge.

Then in 1990 a world ban on trading in elephant parts, from live animals to elephant products (including teeth, hide, feet, flesh, bones, and, of course, ivory) became law. For the thousands of Asian carvers, the supply of legal African ivory ended. So, instead, many carvers worked on **smuggled** African ivory and newly poached Asian ivory. Some continue to do so today.

Today most western people would rather go without ivory than support this trade. However, some markets for ivory are growing. In Japan, for example, ivory *hanko*—personal name stamps—are increasingly popular. In China and the Middle East, too, people are buying more carved ivory than before.

Ban or no ban?

Not all conservationists agree on how best to tackle the ivory trade. Some people think that traders and carvers should be allowed to sell a small amount of ivory each year. Some of the money raised can be channeled to elephant conservation projects. Others argue that this system would be too complicated and give out the wrong message— that it is all right to collect ivory. They say only a total ban will make the public realize that ivory belongs on the elephant, and put poachers out of business. Another possibility is to encourage Asia's ivory carvers to work in other materials, such as bone, jade, or stone.

Out of balance

Ivory poachers usually target the elephants with the largest tusks—that is to say, mature bulls. The result is that heavily poached populations are running low on mature bulls. It is a particular problem in southern India. The reserves of Bandipur—Mudumalai contain 1 bull to every 12 to 15 cows, while the Periyar Tiger Reserve contains 1 to every 100. With so few bulls, **breeding** is slow and population starts to drop.

Captives in Crisis

It is not just wild elephants that are losing the fight for survival. There are also threats facing the tame elephants that make up as much as a third of the total Asian elephant population.

Why keep elephants today?

In all countries where elephants live in the wild, except in Myanmar (Burma), capturing elephants is now illegal (it was banned in India in 1973). However, in small numbers, elephants still fulfill a variety of roles. Some countries, such as Myanmar (Burma) and India, still use their tame elephants for **logging,** since the animals can work in mountains where vehicles cannot go.

*Tourists in Royal Chitwan National Park, Nepal, take an elephant ride to view an even rarer **native** animal— the one-horned rhinoceros.*

Many elephants are still used in entertainment and tourism, though they are monitored closely by animal rights groups. In India, for example, elephants are kept in zoos, perform in circuses, and are kept in private collections, some of which use their animals as tourist attractions.

Efforts are underway to have all elephant owners register their animals with the authorities. The information, stored on computers, will enable conservationists to manage populations, keep accurate counts, and monitor any cases of animal abuse. Currently fewer than half of India's captive elephants are registered.

Out-of-work elephants

A decline in the forestry industry has meant less work for tame elephants. Many elephants that were once busy in the timber camps are now out of work. Thailand, for example, has lost about three quarters of its forest area since 1900. Thailand banned the use of elephants in logging in 1989, and now these few animals are mostly out of work.

Desperate keepers earned money by making their elephants perform tricks for tourists in cities. The elephants were poorly cared for. In 2002 the Thai government banned elephants from cities. This has merely shifted the problem to the back roads and tourist sites, where **mahouts** beg for handouts.

An Asian keeper traditionally ties up his elephant with chains to keep it from wandering and to make it easier to handle. Many people now feel that this method of restraint is cruel.

Hard to handle

Elephants are difficult to maintain. Until recent decades up to half of elephants died in the first week of captivity. A common cause of death was overworked heart muscles. When their bulls came into **musth** and became hard to restrain, some keepers would shackle their feet and give them powerful drugs or poisons, often killing them. As late as the 20th century, vets were still recommending the drug opium, or poisons like arsenic and strychnine, for medicinal use.

Health problems are a key issue as the world's captive Asian elephant population enters old age. Even today, with modern medicine, tame elephants suffer foot and skin infections if they are not exercised and groomed regularly. Without a proper diet they suffer vitamin deficiency. They need space to roam and the company of others.

The Zoo Debate

This elephant is kept in a zoo in Alaska. Weather conditions like this are far from ideal for an animal that is used to hot climates.

Keeping large **mammals** in zoos is never easy. Visitors to modern zoos want to see animals kept in conditions as near to natural as possible. But a report on European zoos published in 2002 revealed that elephants are still being mistreated. For example, the report found that herds in zoos are too small. Cows are kept apart—sometimes permanently—from their calves and sisters. Even the best enclosures are up to a hundred times smaller than **home ranges** in the wild.

Zoo elephants often suffer from health problems. Because of the cold, wet weather in **temperate** countries, elephants there may be kept indoors for up to 16 hours a day. The lack of exercise and an unbalanced diet mean that cows are up to 70 percent heavier than their wild counterparts. Damp conditions and hard floors lead to the early onset of **arthritis.** Some 40 percent of zoo elephants show some form of upset behavior—for example, treading the same path again and again, or endlessly weaving the head from side to side. It is no surprise then that an Asian elephant's average life span in a zoo is only 15 years.

Number of registered captive Asian elephants

The International Species Information System (ISIS), an international nonprofit organization, and the Captive Elephant Database (CED), run by elephant keepers, both list the animals kept in zoos and similar institutions. These numbers do not include thousands of unregistered tame elephants.

Continent	Zoos & safari parks	Circuses	Working camps & private owners
Europe	330	184	0
North and Central America	210	184	14
Asia	79+	11	8
Africa	5+	3	0
Australia	10	9	0
South America	0+	0	0
World total	**634+**	**391**	**22**

Why keep elephants in zoos?

The managers of zoos claim that keeping elephants offers many benefits, including better elephant research. Biologists can study the elephants at close quarters. By claiming that the elephants are for research purposes, zoos can obtain a rare legal permit to **import** elephants. Zoo supporters also point to the fact that admission charges from zoo visitors help pay for conservation programs in the elephants' **range countries.** Watching elephants close up allows us to learn more about them, and stirs our interest in conservation. Matching **breeding** pairs allows conservationists to sustain **genetic diversity** and breed animals to be reintroduced into the wild.

Opponents of zoos dispute these claims. Though zoo elephants are certainly useful, biologists could also study orphans or working elephants in **logging** camps. Elephants are actually very expensive to house in zoos, and this cost must be contrasted with the amount of money they raise in admission charges. People do not need to see captive elephants in order to be persuaded to make donations. There is little educational value to be had from seeing poorly kept or ill elephants. Furthermore, elephants do not breed well in captivity. It is 50 times cheaper to manage herds in the wild than to keep similar numbers in zoos.

As wild herds dwindle, the debate over keeping elephants in zoos continues.

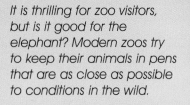

It is thrilling for zoo visitors, but is it good for the elephant? Modern zoos try to keep their animals in pens that are as close as possible to conditions in the wild.

Conserving Asian Elephants

Because there are many different threats to the Asian elephant, conservation needs action on many fronts.

Elephants and the law

The Asian elephant is on Appendix I to CITES, the Convention on International Trade in Endangered Species of Wild Fauna and Flora. Any animal listed on Appendix I cannot be traded internationally without a special license. When CITES was created in 1975, the Asian elephant was among the first animals on Appendix. One of the most important laws protecting elephants in India is the Wildlife Act, first introduced in 1972. India has upgraded the 1972 act several times. In 1978, for example, it banned export of the Asian elephant, and in 1986 it banned the **ivory** trade within India. Another important law was the ban on the international trade in ivory. Since it came into effect in 1990, the ban has helped stabilize elephant numbers in both Africa and Asia. In 1997 the United States passed the Asian Elephant Conservation Act, and has since donated several million dollars to more than 40 different elephant conservation projects.

Conserving habitat

Currently, of the 170,000 sq mi (440,000 sq km) where Asian elephants still live, just over 5,000 sq mi (13,000 sq km) lie within reserves or sanctuaries. Though these areas are still targeted by **poachers,** illegal loggers, or farmers, some protection is better than none. About 2,000 Asian elephants live in India's Kaziranga National Park and the Nagaland hills. In southern India, over 1,100 Asian elephants live in the Periyar Tiger Reserve. At Periyar, and in the Nagarhole National Park, Bandipur Tiger Reserve, and Mudumalai Sanctuary, there are 1 to 3 elephants per every 0.5 sq mi (1.3 sq km).

In Thailand there are 4 major protected areas for elephants. Khao

A calf feeds from its mother in the Kaziranga National Park, India.

Yai National Park is home to about 225 elephants. The existing protected area covers over 9,600 square miles (25,000 square kilometers). It is home to only 50 percent of the wild elephants that live in the country. Chinese elephants are confined to the **tropical** forests of Xishuangbanna Nature Reserve, in Yunnan province.

Flagships

A flagship **species** is one that people care a lot about. Increasingly, governments and conservation organizations are focusing their work on preserving areas rich in animals, such as elephants, tigers, or rhinoceroses where there is strong support from local residents and the wider public. Protecting a flagship species is a very effective way of saving an entire wildlife hotspot from destruction.

Corridors

To link isolated elephant populations, conservationists create green corridors of elephant-friendly terrain between key **habitat** areas. In Thailand, for example, the Royal Forest Department is working with local people to create a corridor between two protected areas, the Ang Luenai Wildlife Sanctuary and Khao Chamao National Park. It is a situation that helps everyone: the elephants get living space, while the local farmers keep their crops elephant-free. The World Land Trust has also begun a project to link protected areas in northeast India with three corridors. The Siju-Rewak elephant corridor will put about 20 percent of the world's Asian elephants (around 9,200 animals) in contact with each other.

The WWF and AREAS

The World Wildlife Fund (WWF) is currently running an Asian Rhino and Elephant Area Strategy (AREAS). The AREAS program has identified eight elephant priority landscapes spread over seven **range countries**. WWF is trying to establish new national parks and reserves in the priority landscapes, promote better use of natural **resources**, and improve anti-poaching measures. Many other rare **mammals** are likely to benefit from AREAS, including the tiger, sun bear, sloth bear, clouded leopard, and Ganges river dolphin.

WWF's elephant priority landscapes:

India	Nilgiris/Eastern Ghats
	Kaziranga/Karbi-Anglong
	Arunachal/Assam/Namdapha
Thailand	Tenasserim/
	Western Forest Complex
Malaysia/Indonesia	south Sabah/
	northeast Kalimantan
Malaysia/Thailand	Hala Bala National Park/
	Taman Negara National Park
Indonesia	Tesso Nilo
Vietnam/Laos/Cambodia	Emerald Triangle

Focus on Sumatra

The plight of Sumatran elephants shows how the conflict between elephants and locals is placing a growing burden on governments. **Tropical** lowland **rain forest** once covered almost all of Sumatra, one of the largest Indonesian islands. In some places, swampy and in others, mountainous, the forest provided a vast **habitat** for the island's orangutans, tigers, rhinos, and elephants. After World War II, the government began moving millions of Indonesian people from the heavily overcrowded islands of Java, Bali, and Madera to Sumatra and other islands. Since then, forest has been cleared to make way for the settlers and their crops, which include rice, rubber, and coffee.

There has also been a rapid growth of commercial **logging** and farming on Sumatra over the last 50 years. Much of the logging is illegal and almost impossible for the authorities to control. **Plantations** of oil palms and softwood trees are replacing the forest so rapidly that it is feared the island will lose all of its lowland rain forest by 2010. New roads, oil and gas wells, mines, and forest fires only add to the threats facing Sumatra's remaining wild places.

As elephant habitat on Sumatra is slashed to make way for crop plantations, refugee elephants like these are flooding the island's rescue centers. They simply cannot cope with the high numbers.

Elephant threats

This loss of habitat has splintered the Sumatran elephant's populations. By the 1990s there were an estimated 44 separate populations. Only 15 of these were thought to contain more than 100 elephants. Elephants are being forced into new and unfamiliar **ranges,** alarming local people. Fishers, for example, have been setting spear traps and shooting or poisoning elephants simply because they do not want the animals around. Other elephants have been made homeless by the relentless clearing of forest.

Rescue centers

The Indonesian government rescues Sumatran elephants that have been made homeless or threatened by locals. Since the 1980s it has been trying to transfer them from problem areas to wildernesses, but suitable habitat is running out fast. In the meantime, rescued animals are housed in special camps. From 1991 to 2001 alone, 500 elephants were taken into centers on the island. But many of the centers cannot afford to care for their animals or the environment.

For example, a survey in 2000 found that the Sebanga-Duri Center in Riau, Sumatra, had a monthly veterinary budget of only one dollar per elephant, a figure far short of what is required. Most of the elephants were getting sick from an unbalanced diet and poisonous drinking water. Farmers, loggers, and oil palm planters had illegally taken over 80 percent of the center's original land.

In an attempt to cut the costs of running the centers, the government is asking tourist operators, logging companies, zoos, and conservation centers to take the rescued elephants. So far they have managed to rehouse more than 250 animals. But overall the program has not been a great success. Like the government, private companies find elephant keeping too expensive.

*The Sumatran elephant is also known as the pocket elephant because it is smaller than most other **subspecies**. Sadly, there are only small areas of its habitat available.*

Helping People Help Asian Elephants

About half of the Asian elephant's remaining **range** is likely to be lost by 2050 unless action is taken. It is up to governments to crack down on illegal loggers and **plantation** owners, and to research nondestructive ways of exploiting forests.

Creating new reserves and linking corridors, as well as strengthening protection of existing areas, is essential. However, with so many rural people in desperate need of natural **resources,** it is wrong to put the elephants' needs first. The challenge is to find solutions that benefit both elephants and people. These include, for example, moving bulls from where they are causing problems and introducing them to herds that need mature bulls.

Crop raiders and other troublesome elephants can be moved. This **tranquilized** elephant is being nudged into a truck by domestic elephants, which also have a calming effect on the wild animal.

New homes for troublemakers

Translocation involves taking a particularly troublesome elephant from one area and moving it to new **habitat.** It is an expensive method, involving fencing, wardening, and the creation of special corridors of land. Often the elephant does not settle in its new home and tries to leave—but the idea can work. Sugar cane planters on Sumatra successfully drove an entire herd of 70 elephants from crop land to a nearby game reserve in 1984–1985.

Turning poachers into protectors

In many regions there is a strong link between villagers and **poachers.** Villagers who have suffered from elephant raids are happy for poachers to remove what they see as the cause of their misfortune.

One way to break this link is to pay villagers **compensation** money for lost crops or family members killed by elephants. This requires a great deal of organization, and sometimes a government cannot afford to pay. In the Xishuangbanna reserve in China, for example, a tiny elephant population—fewer than 200—caused over $2 million worth of damage to crops and rubber trees during 2001. That year, however, the government had a total fund of only $95,000 to hand out.

Another way to involve locals in the fight against poaching is to train them to work as antipoaching **wardens.** That way, they are paid to protect the elephant. Local people can also find work as rangers, tour guides, and research assistants.

Creating a caring generation

None of these changes will succeed without teaching people to care about elephants. In India the Center for Environment Education has designed workbooks for students, and posters and handbooks for teachers that help 10- to 14-year-old students learn about the Asian elephant. The package is being sent to hundreds of schools in India, Sri Lanka, and Bangladesh.

Students in Sri Lanka pay a visit to an elephant orphanage. An experience like this can teach young people that elephants are an important part of their culture.

It might seem that unless you live in one of its **range countries**, you can do nothing to help the Asian elephant. However, there are ways you can change how people treat the environment in Asia. this will help the elephant.

Save the forests

Saving Asian forests can help save elephants—not to mention orangutans, rhinos, proboscis monkeys, and other rare animals. The United States **imports** about $450 million worth of timber from Indonesia. A significant amount of this is illegally harvested, then snuck into the United States by way of Singapore.

Ask before you buy

Ask your parents to make sure they buy products—picture frames and wooden furniture, for example—made from legally harvested timber. Stores should be able to explain where they get their items from, and assure customers that it is legal. If your parents buy timber for jobs around the house, they should look for the green Forest Stewardship Council (FSC) logo on the timber; this shows that the timber comes from a managed forest. The FSC is an international timber watchdog organization based in Mexico.

This tiny orphan elephant is cared for at Kaziranga National Park. It was rescued by the Wildlife Trust of India.

Join a support group

There are many conservation organizations worldwide helping to save both Asian and African elephants. Most of them depend on people giving them money to support their activities. When you pay your membership to join a group that supports elephant conservation projects, you are contributing to their funds. You can also help raise funds by organizing an awareness event for the organization of your choice.

Kuala Gandah in Malaysia is one of many field centers in Asia working to save the elephant. Their first step is to raise money and public awareness.

There are plenty of organizations to choose from. The IFAW (International Fund for Animal Welfare) has an Asian and African elephant campaign. The Elephant Family brings together experts in Asian elephant biology and conservation in projects in the elephants' range countries. Friends of the Asian Elephant is concerned with the welfare of Thailand's elephants. The Elephant Help Project is another Thai elephant conservation program. The Malaysian Elephant Appeal funds the care of animals held at the Kuala Gandah Elephant Center in Malaysia.

IFAW

INTERNATIONAL FUND FOR ANIMAL WELFARE
WWW.IFAW.ORG

ossary

arthritis   painful swelling of the body's joints

bachelor   single male

breed   produce offspring (babies)

browse   foliage and woody material, especially twigs and bark, from plants; also to eat such material

circumference   length of the line that forms a circle

compensate   repay someone for a loss or injury

crèche   where young are kept in a group and cared for by a few adults

deforestation   destruction of a forest

digest   break down food in the stomach and intestines and take in nutrients

DNA   (deoxyribonucleic acid), a chemical inside cells that forms instructions called genes, telling cells how to work and grow

evaporate   turn from liquid into vapor

fallow   land that is left unplanted after a crop has been harvested there

floodplain   riverside area that is regularly drenched or flooded by the river, typically rich in nutrients deposited from the water

genetic diversity   when individuals in a group have inherited different genes

germinate   when a seed sprouts and begins to grow

gland   body organ that releases a particular substance that helps the body work

gut   stomach and canal through which food passes in order to be digested

habitat   animal's natural living space

home range   area within which an animal lives and which supplies all the animal's needs

hormone   chemical in the body that can affect mood and health

humid   damp

import   bring in from another country

ivory   hard, creamy-white substance making up most of an elephant's tusk

logging   harvesting trees for commercial use

mahout   Hindi word for trained elephant rider and keeper

malaria   disease in humans carried by mosquitoes that causes fever and can kill

mammal   warm-blooded animal that feeds its young on milk from the mother's body

mate   when two animals get together to produce offspring, or a partner with which an animal can produce offspring

matriarch   female who is accepted as leader of the herd because of her great age and experience

migration   regular seasonal movement of an animal, usually made across land or up and down hills

molar   cheek tooth, usually with a ridged crown (top) for grinding food

monsoon   seasonal wind in Asia that brings heavy rainfall; also describes rainy season itself

musth   condition in which a bull elephant's body prepares for mating and his behavior becomes more excitable and aggressive

native   belonging to a specified place; one who belongs to that place

nutritious   food that contains chemicals that help a body grow and function

organism   living body

peninsula   long piece of land that sticks out like a finger into a sea or ocean

plantation   large field containing a single crop planted in lines or rows

poach   hunt illegally

predator   animal that hunts and kills other animals

prehistoric   time before humans started leaving a record of their existence

radio transmitter   device that sends out a radio signal

rain forest   leafy forest that grows wherever annual rainfall is higher than about 100 inches (250 centimeters)

range   overall area where a wildlife species is found

range country   country where elephants live

resource   thing that can be useful

satellite   spacecraft circling Earth; some are used to bounce radio signals from one place to another

scrub   rough terrain dotted with stunted clumps of plant life

smuggle   transport something illegally to sell

species   scientific name for a particular kind of plant, animal, or other living thing. Two individuals of the same species can reproduce and have babies. Individuals from separate species cannot.

submissive   accepting a lower rank than another member of one's own group

subspecies   population of animals or other living things that differs slightly from others of the same species. Subspecies are usually restricted to a particular geographical area.

temperate   climate that features winters and summers without extremes of temperature

thicket   area of overgrown shrubs

tranquilize   make calm, stable, or unconscious with the use of chemicals

tropical   moist and very warm climate

vegetation   plants

warden   person who is employed to protect a place or an animal

Conservation groups

Friends of the Asian Elephant
Find out about the welfare of Thailand's Asian elephants.

350 Moo 8, Ram-Indra Road, Soi 61 (KM.6.) Tharneng,
Bangkhen, Bangkok 10230
Thailand

The Elephant Sanctuary
Sick and needy elephants are cared for at this home in
Tennessee.

P.O.Box 393
Hohenwald, TN 38462

The Malaysian Elephant Appeal
This group funds the care of animals held at the Kuala Gandah
Elephant Center in Malaysia.

c/o Asiaprima, 51, Jalan Industri 4,
Taman Perindustrian Temerloh,
28400 Mentakab, Pahang
Malaysia

Worldwide Fund for Nature (WWF)
Find out more about WWF's elephant projects in southeastern Asia.

1250 24th Street NW
Washington DC 20037-1175

Books

Buckley, Carol. *Travels with Tarra*. Gardiner, Maine: Tilbury House, 2002.

Darling, Kathy. *The Elephant Hospital*. Brookfield, Conn.: Millbrook Press, 2002.

Meeker, Clare Hodgson. *Hansa: The True Story of an Asian Elephant Baby*. Seattle: Sasquatch Books, 2003.

Smith, Roland. *In the Forest with the Elephants*. Minneapolis: Sagebrush Education Resources, 1998.

Solway, Andrew. *Classifying Mammals*. Chicago: Heinemann Library, 2003.

Spilsbury, Richard, and Louise Spilsbury. *A Herd of Elephants*. Chicago: Heinemann Library, 2004.

Travers, Will. *Elephant*. Chicago: Raintree, 2000.

Index